Dominican Americans

KAREN PRICE HOSSELL

Heinemann Library
Chicago, Illinois

Customer Service 888-454-2279

Visit our website at www.heinemannlibrary.com

Designed by Roslyn Broder
Photo research by Scott Braut
Printed in China by WKT Company Limited

08 07 06 05 04
10 9 8 7 6 5 4 3 2 1

Library of Congress Cataloging-in-Publication Data
Price Hossell, Karen, 1957-
   Dominican Americans / Karen Price Hossell.
      p. cm. -- (We are America)
   Summary: An overview of the history and daily lives of Dominican people who immigrated to the United States.
   Includes bibliographical references and index.
   ISBN 1-4034-5020-X
 1. Dominican Americans--Juvenile literature. 2. Immigrants--United States--Juvenile literature. 3. United States--Emigration and immigration--Juvenile literature. 4. Dominican Republic--Emigration and immigration--Juvenile literature. 5. Dominican Americans--Biography--Juvenile literature. 6. Immigrants--United States--Biography--Juvenile literature. [1. Dominican Americans.] I. Title. II. Series.
   E184.D6P75 2004
   973'.04687293--dc22
                              2003021700

Acknowledgments
The author and publisher are grateful to the following for permission to reproduce copyright material:
pp. 4, 5, 28 Courtesy of Nelly Rosario; pp. 7, 17, 20, 22, 24, 26 Martha Cooper; p. 8 Hulton-Deutsch Collection/Corbis; p. 9 Bettmann/Corbis; pp. 10, 11, 14, 18 Scott Braut; p. 12 AP Wide World Photos; p. 15 Richard B. Levine; p. 16 Rudi Von Briel/Photo Edit; p. 19 Jonathan Daniel/Getty Images; p. 21 Michael Newman/Photo Edit; p. 23 Madeline Polss/Envision; p. 25 Mary Altaffer/AP Wide World Photo; p. 27 Robert Brenner/Photo Edit; p. 29 Jerry Bauer

Cover photographs by Michael Newman/PhotoEdit, (background) Rudi Von Briel/Photo Edit

Special thanks to Silvio Torres-Saillant, associate professor of English and director of Latino-Latin American Studies Program at Syracuse University, for his comments made in preparation of this book. Karen Price Hossell wishes to thank Brian Krumm and Nelly Rosario for sharing her story.

Some quotations and material used in this book come from the following source. In some cases, quotes have been abridged for clarity: page 11 reprinted with permission of the *Worcester Telegram & Gazette*.

A Dominican-American family who lives in the Los Angeles, California, area is shown on the cover of this book. A photo of the Washington Heights neighborhood in New York City is shown in the background. Washington Heights has a large Dominican-American population.

Contents

Some words are shown in bold, **like this.** You can find out what they mean by looking in the glossary.

A New Home in New York

Nelly Rosario came to the United States from the Dominican Republic when she was only three months old. Nelly's parents had moved to New York City in the 1960s, but her mother gave birth to Nelly in the Dominican Republic. The Rosarios moved to New York because there were jobs available there. Also, many people there spoke Spanish, like the Rosarios did in the Dominican Republic. As they had with other Dominican **immigrants**, people living in New York helped the Rosarios get **settled.**

Nelly is seen here at a family birthday party in 1973. Her mother Isabel is holding her.

It was hard for the Rosario family to get used to living in New York. The winters there were much colder than in the Dominican Republic. The Rosarios also missed family members still living in the Dominican Republic. After a while, New York started to feel like home. Nelly's father learned to speak English, went to college, and graduated by the time Nelly was eight years old. Her mother got to know others in the neighborhood and became active in the local church **community.**

Nelly is sitting in the middle in this photo. It was taken in the Dominican Republic in 1977.

I remember not being able to speak English, even in kindergarten, since we spoke Spanish at home. And we lived in a **Latino** community, so there was really no pressure to **integrate** outside of our homes.

—Nelly Rosario

The Dominican Republic

The Dominican Republic is a country on an island called Hispaniola in the Caribbean Sea. About nine million people live in the Dominican Republic. The country is about twice as large as the state of New Hampshire. There are many mountains and hills in the Dominican Republic. Many workers there make money by growing sugarcane, coffee, and cocoa and selling them to other countries.

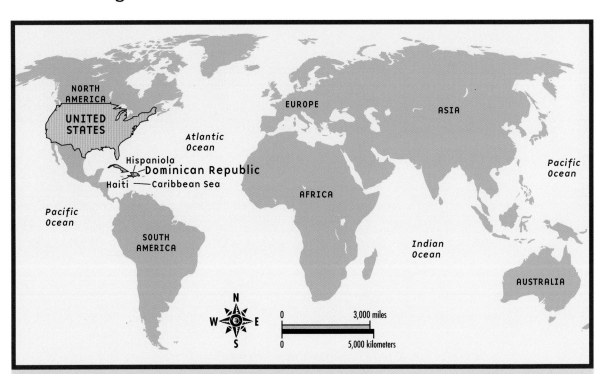

This map shows where the United States and the Dominican Republic are located. A republic is a country in which people vote to elect their leaders.

This photo shows a birthday party at a house in Puerto Plaza, a city in the Dominican Republic. Some children in the photo are performing a Dominican dance called the merengue.

Christopher Columbus landed on Hispaniola on his first voyage to the **New World** in 1492. He set up his headquarters on Hispaniola as he explored the area. The Dominican Republic takes up more than half of the island of Hispaniola. On the rest of the island is the country of Haiti.

The First Dominican Immigrants

In the 1700s and 1800s, some people from Hispaniola island went to the United States. Some of them were women who had married American sailors. But because few records were kept of **immigrants** during those years, it is difficult to say exactly how many Dominicans moved to the U.S. In the 1900s, it was hard for Dominicans to move to the U.S. Dominican government leaders did not want anyone to leave the country.

The **dictator** Rafael Trujillo ruled the Dominican Republic from 1930 until he was **assassinated** in 1961. While he ruled, he did not allow Dominicans to leave the island. Many Dominicans left the country after his death.

Dominican dictator Rafael Trujillo is shown here giving a speech in the Dominican Republic. Many thought he was an unfair leader.

In 1960, these Dominicans gathered in New York City to speak out against Rafael Trujillo. He had recently been accused of trying to have the president of another country killed.

In 1961, it became easier for Dominicans Republic to move out of the country. Thousands of people left to go to the U.S. It made sense to many Dominicans to move to the U.S. because of the long history of relations between the two countries. The Dominican Republic actually almost became part of U.S. territory in the late 1800s.

Time Line

1844   Dominican Republic becomes a country.

1916–1924   United States controls Dominican Republic's government. Many groups there were fighting about which type of government was best for the country.

1930   Rafael Trujillo takes over the government.

1961   Trujillo is assassinated. People are allowed to immigrate.

1961–1970   More than 90,000 people from the Dominican Republic immigrate to the U.S.

2002   About 23,000 Dominicans immigrate to the U.S.

Settling in the United States

The first Dominican **immigrants** usually lived in small apartments in the United States and took whatever jobs they could get. Many of them had only been to school for a few years in the Dominican Republic. They knew they would have to work at low-paying jobs in the U.S. But they thought their children would be able to go to good schools and have more opportunities in life than they did.

Dominican American Mario Martinez moved to the U.S. in 1967 and lived in Salt Lake City, Utah. He now owns a sporting goods store in New York City's Washington Heights neighborhood.

Some of the first Dominican immigrants opened businesses, such as this Dominican bakery in Washington Heights, New York City.

Many of these early immigrants **settled** in New York City in two neighborhoods, Corona and Washington Heights. Some went to the city of Lawrence, Massachusetts, which is near Boston. In these areas, some Dominican immigrants opened stores known as **bodegas.** The store owners had food and other items brought in from the Dominican Republic. Dominican immigrants opened other businesses, as well. Some felt that it was easier to open their own businesses than to find jobs working for others.

We came to America because we wanted a better life, and I think we've found it.
—Ana Martinez, who moved from the Dominican Republic to Worcester, Massachusetts, in 1983

Dominican Immigration Today

Between 1961 and 1986, about 400,000 Dominicans **immigrated** to the United States. Today, Dominicans continue to move to the U.S. Many move to find better jobs and schools than they could in the Dominican Republic. Some Dominicans move because they believe that living conditions, such as housing and the supply of water and electrical power, are better in the U.S.

*Some Dominicans tried to enter the United States **illegally**, like this group shown in 1986. Their boat was seized by the U.S. Coast Guard.*

Dominican Immigration to the United States

This map shows some of the cities and states that Dominican immigrants first moved to and where many still live today.

Dominican Americans who immigrated to the United States in the 1960s and 1970s often help new immigrants from the Dominican Republic today. When new immigrants arrive, Dominican Americans often give them advice about how to find a job and where to live. There are also organizations in the U.S., such as the Latin American **Integration** Center in New York, that help Dominican immigrants get **settled.**

Yesterday and Today

Some Dominicans who moved to the United States in the 1960s and 1970s had a hard time getting used to their new lives. Some were treated unfairly by other Americans. Possibly for this reason, Dominican **immigrants settled** in the same neighborhoods in the U.S. and formed their own **communities.** In the 1980s, Dominican Americans also opened factories and other businesses, and they gave newly arrived Dominicans jobs working there.

This photo shows a street in New York City's Washington Heights neighborhood, which is known as the "Little Dominican Republic."

Alianza Dominicana is an organization in New York that some Dominican immigrants go to for help in getting settled and finding jobs after they move to the U.S.

Today, there are groups run by Dominican Americans to help not only new immigrants but also those who have lived in the U.S. for a while. Some groups help Dominican-American businesspeople, students, doctors, and others as they develop careers. Other groups celebrate Dominican **culture.** These groups hold festivals, dances, and concerts that feature Dominican music, dancing, and food.

Dominican Americans have been elected to serve in state governments. They include William Lantigua, Massachusetts; Carlos Gonzalez, New Hampshire; Adriano Espaillat, New York; and Juan Pichardo, Rhode Island.

The Way of Life in the United States

By the 1980s, large numbers of Dominican Americans were living in neighborhoods in New York City. Many were also were living in Miami, Florida, and northern New Jersey. Today, Dominican Americans own many businesses in these neighborhoods. Dominican flags are displayed in store windows. **Bodegas** sell Dominican food and Spanish-language newspapers. Many travel agencies in the neighborhoods give special rates on trips to the Dominican Republic.

This photo shows some businesses owned by Dominican Americans in New York City's Little Dominican Republic neighborhood.

16

This group of Dominican-American children read a story to each other in their classroom in New York.

Because they formed tight-knit **communities** in these areas, many have found that they can continue to live there much as they did in the Dominican Republic. They speak Spanish, read Spanish newspapers, and watch Spanish television programs. Often, Dominican-American children in large cities are put into **bilingual** classrooms. The children learn English from their teachers and from one another. Some Dominican-American parents then learn English from their children.

U.S. Cities with Largest Dominican-American Populations

City	Number of Dominican Americans
New York City	424,847
Miami, Florida	36,454
Bergen-Passaic, New Jersey	36,360
Jersey City, New Jersey	27,709
Boston, Massachusetts	25,057

Jobs

Dominican Americans work at the same kinds of jobs that other Americans do. Many of the people who **immigrated** in the 1980s and 1990s work at jobs in factories. Some Dominican-American women work as housekeepers, **nannies,** and cooks. Dominican Americans whose parents immigrated in the 1960s and 1970s usually attend college after graduating from high school. Many have become doctors, writers, scientists, and artists.

Sara Aponte works as a librarian in the Dominican Studies Institute. The institute is part of the City College of New York.

Sammy Sosa, a Dominican-American baseball player, plays for the Chicago Cubs. He started playing baseball as a boy growing up in the Dominican Republic.

Many young boys in the Dominican Republic dream of playing **professional** baseball in the United States. They spend hours practicing. Some cannot even afford to buy baseball bats, so they use sticks instead. American baseball teams such as the Los Angeles Dodgers have camps in the Dominican Republic where coaches train young men to be major-league players. Probably the most famous Dominican baseball player in the U.S. is Sammy Sosa. Other Dominican players include Pedro Martinez and Alex Rodriguez.

Homes and Families

Home life is important to most Dominican Americans. As children, they often learn about Dominican **culture** and history at home. Most Dominican Americans enjoy living in the United States and love being Americans. But they also like to remember the **traditions** of their homeland. At home, they might speak Spanish, listen to Dominican music, and eat meals made with food that is popular in the Dominican Republic.

This Dominican-American family was photographed in front of a Christmas tree. Many Dominican-American families have gatherings in their homes to celebrate holidays.

Dominican-American families like this one live all over the United States, especially in New York, Florida, New Jersey, and Massachusetts.

Sometimes, relatives in Dominican-American families live in the same houses or neighborhoods. Newly arrived **immigrants** might stay with a Dominican-American family until they find jobs and places to live. When they find jobs, they often send money back to family members in the Dominican Republic. The money might be used to buy food or other items, or family members might use the money to immigrate to the United States themselves.

As a group, we have kept ties to our culture and language, as well to the importance of family.
—Nelly Rosario, speaking about Dominican Americans in general

Dominican Food

Dominican Americans enjoy all the foods that other Americans eat. But they enjoy Dominican foods as well. In Dominican-American neighborhoods, Dominican foods are sold in local stores. The most common meal in the Dominican Republic is rice and beans. Many Dominican Americans have a meal of rice and beans once a day.

Dominican Americans also enjoy food commonly served in the United States. This Dominican-American mother and daughter had pizza for lunch in New York City.

This Dominican dish is called el sancocho. *It is often served with a side dish of rice.*

Another popular Dominican dish is *el sancocho.* This is a stew made with meat, potatoes, bananas, corn, tomatoes, and **plantains.** A typical Dominican meal might also include fish, plantains, and **cassava** bread. *El mambá* is a spread similar to peanut butter. It is popular in some parts of the Dominican Republic. *El mambá* is made from boiled peanuts mixed with hot pepper or salt.

Holidays and Celebrations

Dominican Americans celebrate many of the same holidays that other Americans do. One special holiday is Dominican **Independence** Day on February 27. The day celebrates and observes the Dominican Republic gaining its independence from Haiti. Several cities in the United States have celebrations for Dominican Independence Day.

These Dominican-American girls wore dresses that featured the colors of the flag of the Dominican Republic. They were in a parade for Dominican Independence Day.

These Dominican Americans wore costumes and masks in a parade in New York City as part of a celebration of Dominican Independence Day.

To celebrate Dominican Independence Day, many Dominican Americans attend concerts and parades. There are also street fairs with carnival rides and booths that sell Dominican foods. Boston, Seattle, Atlanta, Miami, and New York City are some of the cities that have celebrations for Dominican Independence Day.

Music and Dancing

Like other Americans, many Dominican Americans enjoy music and dancing. One very popular style of Dominican music and dancing is called merengue. One instrument played in merengue music is the guiro. A guiro is a hollow **gourd** with notches that a musician scrapes with a stick. Other instruments include a double-sided drum called a *tambora* and the *marimbula,* a hollow, wooden box with pieces of metal fastened to it. The metal pieces are plucked to make musical notes.

Dancing is a popular activity for many Dominican-American girls and boys. This girl danced in a parade in New York City.

Some of the people in this picture are holding instruments used in Dominican music, including **maracas** *and a tambora.*

Bachata is a slower kind of Dominican music. *Bachata* songs tell stories that are often romantic and sad. The main instrument in *bachata* is the guitar. Other instruments used to play it are claves, bongos, and guiros. Bongos are a pair of connected drums that are usually played by hand. Claves are a pair of wooden sticks beat together to keep time. *Salsa* is another kind of popular music and dance in the Dominican Republic.

Nelly Rosario Today

Today, Nelly Rosario lives in New York City, where she is a writer. She earned a **degree** from Columbia University, and she teaches there part-time. Nelly has received several awards for her writing. In 2002, her first book was published. The book is called *Song of the Water Saints.* It is about a family living in the Dominican Republic and their move to New York. Nelly knew she wanted to be writer from a young age.

Nelly is shown here at Brooklyn Technical High School in New York on her high-school graduation day. She graduated in 1990.

Nelly goes back to visit the Dominican Republic about every five years and hopes to go even more often in the future. She loves the smells, the sun, the beaches, the music, and the faces and the speech of the people there. But like many Dominican Americans, she also thinks of the United States as her home.

This photo of Nelly was taken in 2002, the same year her book was published. In 2003, the book was published in Spanish as well.

There are many opportunities available here, such as education, jobs, and quality of living, all of which, unfortunately, are not always available in many other parts of the world.

—Nelly Rosario

Dominican Immigration Chart

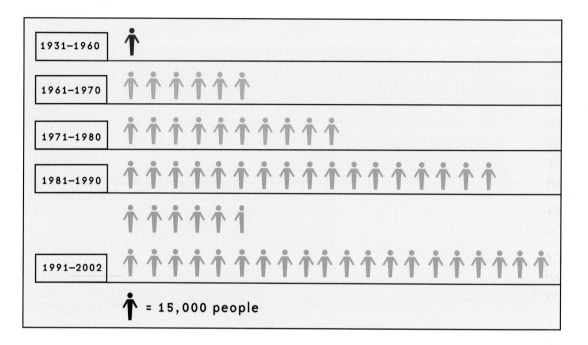

1931–1960	🧍
1961–1970	🧍🧍🧍🧍🧍🧍
1971–1980	🧍🧍🧍🧍🧍🧍🧍🧍🧍🧍
1981–1990	🧍🧍🧍🧍🧍🧍🧍🧍🧍🧍🧍🧍🧍🧍🧍🧍
1991–2002	🧍🧍🧍🧍🧍🧍 🧍🧍🧍🧍🧍🧍🧍🧍🧍🧍🧍🧍🧍🧍🧍🧍🧍🧍

🧍 = 15,000 people

The largest number of Dominican people moved to the United States in the 1990s.

Source: U.S. Immigration and Naturalization Service

More Books to Read

Alvarez, Julia. *Before We Were Free.* New York: Knopf, 2002.

Landau, Elaine. *Dominican Republic.* San Francisco: Children's Book Press, 2000.

Radcliffe, Barbara. *The Dominican Republic.* San Francisco: Children's Book Press, 1999.

Fiction
Miller-Lachmann, Lyn, ed. *Once Upon a Cuento.* Willimantic, Conn.: Curbstone Press, 2003.

Glossary

assassinate to kill a important person by secret or surprise attack

bilingual spoken or used in two languages, such as English and Spanish

bodega store that sells groceries and other goods in Spanish-speaking neighborhoods in the United States

cassava plant with roots that can be cooked and eaten

community group of people with common interests and traditions who live together

culture ideas, skills, arts, and way of life for a certain group of people

degree title a student earns after finishing a program of study at a college or university

dictator ruler with complete power over a country

gourd fruit that grows on a vine. Gourds are similar to pumpkins and melons.

illegal against the law

immigrate to come to a country to live there for a long time. A person who immigrates is an immigrant.

independence condition of being free from the rule of other countries, governments, or people

integrate to blend in or unite

Latino person who comes from or whose relatives come from Latin America, which is Brazil and the Spanish-speaking countries south of the United States

maraca musical instrument made from a gourd filled with seeds or pebbles. It is usually played in pairs by shaking.

nanny person who takes care of small children in a house

New World another name for the place now called the Americas, which is the land of North America, South America, and Central America

plantain plant similar to a banana that has fruit that can be eaten when cooked

professional taking part in an activity, such as a sport, for pay

settle to make a home for yourself and others

tradition belief or practice handed down through the years from one generation to the next

Index